WHO WAS...?

Samuel Pepys

Paul Harrison

First published in 2007 by Wayland
Copyright © Wayland 2007

Wayland
338 Euston Road
London NW1 3BH

Wayland Australia
Level 17/207 Kent Street
Sydney, NSW 2000

Editor: Victoria Brooker
Designer: Jane Stanley

Harrison, Paul, 1969-
    Who was Samuel Pepys?
    1. Pepys, Samuel, 1633-1703 - Juvenile literature
    2. Diarists - England - Biography - Juvenile literature
    3. Statesmen - England - Biography - Juvenile literature
    4. Great Britain - History - Charles II, 1660-1685 -
    Juvenile literature
    I. Title
    942'.066'092
ISBN 978 0 7502 5198 3
Printed in China
Wayland is a division of Hachette Children's Books, an Hachette Livre UK Company.

For permission to reproduce the following pictures, the author and publisher would like to thank: British Library: 17; Annebicque Bernard/Corbis Sygma: 20 Edifice/Corbis: 7; Getty Images (Hulton Archive): 1, 5, 9; Huntingdonshire Tourist Office: 6; Kathy Lockley: 21; Maidstone Museum and Art Gallery, Kent,UK/Bridgeman Art Library, London: 16; Museum of London: 11; Collection of the New York Historical Society/ Bridgeman Art Library, London: 10; Museum of London/Bridgeman Art Library: 13; National Portrait Gallery, London/Bridgeman Art Library, London: 4, Cover; Michael Nicholson/Corbis: 15; Private Collection/Bridgeman Art Library, London: 12; Private Collection/ Photo © Christie's Images, London: 18; Yale Center for British Art, Paul Mellon Collection, USA/Bridgeman Art Library, London: 14, 19; Yale Center for British Art, Paul Mellon Fund, USA/Bridgeman Art Library, London 8

Contents

Words in **bold** can be found in the glossary.

Who was Samuel Pepys?

Samuel Pepys lived from 1633 to 1703. He is most famous for the diary he wrote. His diary tells us what life was like when Pepys was alive. The diary includes lots of important events that Pepys saw at that time, such as the **Great Fire of London** and the **Great Plague**.

This painting hangs in the National Portrait Gallery. It was painted when Pepys was 29 years old.

Pepys also had some important jobs. He helped to organise the Royal Navy and was a **Member of Parliament**.

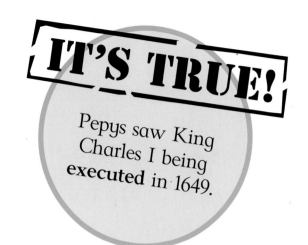

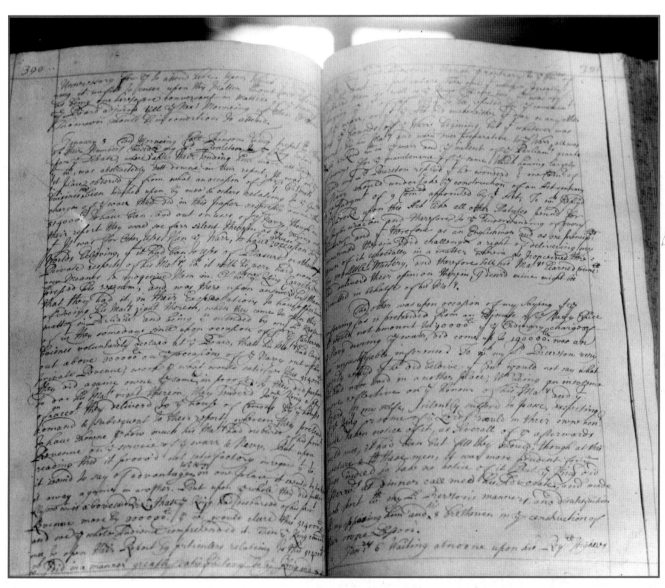

Pepys is best known for his diary.

Early years

Samuel Pepys was born in London on 23 February 1633. For a while he lived in Huntingdonshire with some relatives. In 1646 he returned to London to go to St Paul's School.

The house Pepys stayed at in Huntingdonshire.

He was a bright pupil and was able to go to university. Between 1651 and 1654 he was a student at Magdalene College in Cambridge.

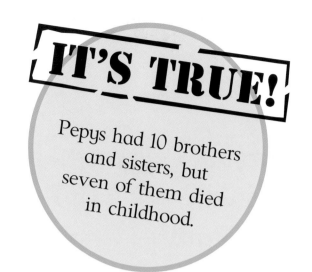

IT'S TRUE!

Pepys had 10 brothers and sisters, but seven of them died in childhood.

Magdalene College, Cambridge.

Work and a wife

Straight after getting his **degree** Pepys started work. His first job was as a **secretary** to a wealthy and powerful man called Edward Montagu. Pepys did well and was soon trusted to look after Montagu's lands and businesses when Edward was away.

In 1660 Montagu was made Earl of Sandwich.

Around this time Pepys fell in love with Elizabeth St Michel. They were married from 1655 until Elizabeth's death in 1669.

Samuel Pepys admires his wife's new dress in this engraving from 1849.

The diary begins

On 1 January 1660, Pepys decided to keep a diary. He didn't know it then but he would record many interesting events. The first big event he saw happened in May 1660 when Charles II became king.

Charles was interested in the arts and sciences and founded the **Royal Society** in 1660.

Pepys's diary shows he was interested in science. In 1665 he became a member of the Royal Society, an organisation interested in mathematics, science and engineering.

Pepys's diary was written using a **quill** dipped in ink.

Plague

In 1665 a deadly disease known as the **Great Plague** hit London. It was very frightening as no one knew how people caught it. Now we know that it was probably passed from person to person by fleas.

There was little that people could do to combat the plague other than leave or pray.

Perhaps as many as 100,000 people died from the plague. Many people fled London, but Pepys stayed and wrote about it in his diary.

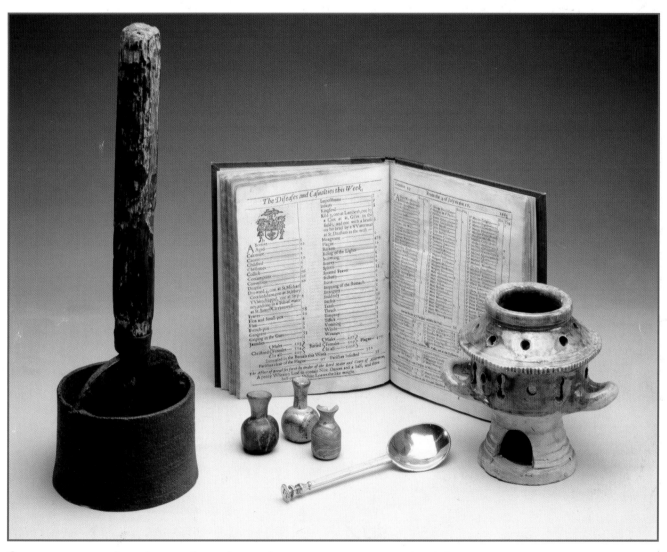

Some people thought the plague was carried in the air and that burning **incense** would kill it.

London's burning

The most famous thing Pepys saw was the **Great Fire of London**. On 2 September 1666 a fire broke out in a bakery on Pudding Lane. The fire burned for four days and destroyed a lot of the city.

London's wooden buildings were quickly destroyed by the flames.

Pepys brought news of the fire to the king. The king asked Pepys to pass on an order to the Mayor to pull down houses to make gaps in the streets. This helped to stop the fire spreading.

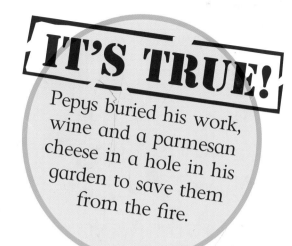

IT'S TRUE!

Pepys buried his work, wine and a parmesan cheese in a hole in his garden to save them from the fire.

The Monument to the Great Fire overlooks the spot where the fire started.

War

During the 1600s Britain went to war against the Dutch three times. Pepys wrote about the Second Dutch War in his diaries. In 1667 he watched the Dutch fleet sail up the Thames and also attack the docks on the Medway river.

The Medway docks burn after the Dutch attack.

Two years later Pepys stopped writing his diary. His eyesight was poor and he thought that writing the diary was making it worse.

Places to Visit

Magdalene College in Cambridge is where the original diaries are kept.

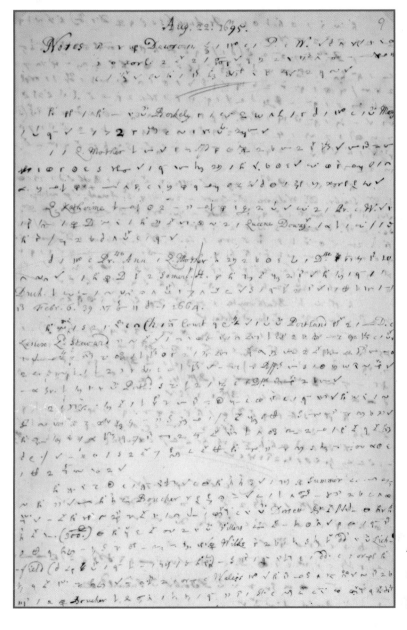

A close up of Pepys's diary shows the **shorthand** he used.

In the Navy

Pepys's day job was to make the Royal Navy work better. He made sure sailors had plenty of food to eat and that ship's captains had been properly **trained**.

Pepys made sure Britain had one of the best navies in the world.

Pepys was also a **Member of Parliament** between 1673 and 1679 and again from 1685 to 1689. Even though he was an M.P. he still worked for the Navy.

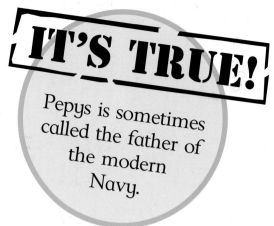

IT'S TRUE!

Pepys is sometimes called the father of the modern Navy.

London in Pepys's time looked very different from the city we know today.

Arrest and death

In 1679 Pepys was arrested because some people thought he was a **traitor**. He was accused of selling secrets to the French and was sent to the Tower of London. He was released after less than two months when it was clear he was innocent. He was arrested again in 1690 but was released after five days.

ENTRY TO THE TRAITORS' GATE

The Tower of London was not just a prison, it was also a royal palace.

In 1701 Pepys retired to Clapham. In those days Clapham was at the edge of London. He died two years later at the age of 70.

Places to Visit

The Museum of London has lots of information on Pepys's London.

Pepys and his wife are buried in St Olave's Church, Hart Street, London.

Timeline

1633	Pepys born in London
1646	Pepys goes to St Paul's School, London
1651	Pepys goes to university at Magdalene College
1654	Pepys graduates from university Starts work for Edward Montagu
1655	Marries Elizabeth St Michel
1660	Starts writing diary
1661	Charles II crowned king
1665	Joins the Royal Society Second Dutch War begins Great Plague hits London
1666	Great Fire of London
1667	Dutch fleet attack Medway Second Dutch War finishes
1669	Stops writing diary Elizabeth dies
1673	Becomes Member of Parliament for Castle Rising
1679	Becomes Member of Parliament for Harwich Arrested and sent to the Tower of London on charges of treason
1684	Becomes President of the Royal Society
1685	Charles II dies Pepys elected M.P. for Harwich for a second time
1690	Pepys put in prison again and then released
1701	Retires to Clapham, London
1703	Pepys dies

Glossary

degree a qualification given to someone who completes their studies at university

executed to be deliberately killed

Great Fire of London the large fire that burnt for four days during 1666 and destroyed much of London

Great Plague in 1665 a disease called the plague arrived in Britain. London was badly affected and many people died

incense spices that smell nice when burnt

Member of Parliament a person voted for by the people to represent them in parliament, where the laws of the land are agreed upon

quill a pen made from a feather

Royal Society an organisation based in London that is interested in mathematics, science and engineering

secretary a person who works for someone else and helps them to do their job, usually by dealing with letters and records

shorthand a quick way of writing using symbols instead of letters and words

trained to learn how to do something properly

traitor someone who betrays a person or country

Further information

Books

The Life of Samuel Pepys by Emma Lynch (Heinemann Library, 2006)

Samuel Pepys's Clerk (History Diaries) by Philip Wooderson (Franklin Watts, 2004)

Websites

http://www.bbc.co.uk/schools/famouspeople/standard/pepys/index.shtml

Write your own name in code with this interactive website from the BBC

http://www.pepys.info/

Read extracts of Pepy's diary and find out more about Edward Monatgu

Index